MARIO LEMIEUX

HOCKEY'S GENTLE GIANT

Jean Sonmor

Macmillan of Canada
A Division of Canada Publishing Corporation
Toronto, Ontario, Canada

Canadian Cataloguing in Publication Data

Sonmor, Jean
　Mario Lemieux, hockey's gentle giant

ISBN 0-7715-9637-5

1. Lemieux, Mario. 2. Hockey players — Canada —
Biography. I. Title.

GV848.5.L45S6 1989　　796.96'2'0924　　C89-094485-7

Art Direction: Steven Baine / Design UYA Inc.
Production Co-ordination: WM Enterprises
Photographs: Bruce Bennett Studios

Produced by Kamin & Howell Inc. for
Macmillan of Canada
A Division of Canada Publishing Corporation
Toronto, Ontario, Canada

Printed in U.S.A.

CONTENTS

CHAPTER ONE
Early Years

"The childhood shows the man as morning shows the day."
— John Milton

On a hot summer's night in 1982 the doorman at the Ports, on Yonge Street in Toronto, did a double take. "Wayne Gretzky is here," someone shouted over the disco din from within. The doorman's hand went quickly to the plush velvet barrier rope that divided the ins from the outs in what was then the hottest disco in the city.

No explanation was necessary. Wayne Gretzky had established himself unequivocally as the greatest hockey player on earth, scoring 92 goals and collecting 212 points in his third NHL season. Such a garish display of greatness brought its own rewards and among them was VIP treatment at the Ports.

Everybody stood back and drank in the aura as the slight, tanned superstar strode toward the bar in the quieter Kon Tiki Room at the back. His entourage followed, but nobody paid much attention beyond noting that he seemed to have a bodyguard with him, a big guy, six-four at least.

A closer look at that "bodyguard" would have revealed a baby face too unformed to be marked by toughness and too young by several years to be in a drinking establishment. Mario Lemieux was just under 16 years old, and this evening with Gretzky was the culmination of what some might describe as a charmed childhood.

At 16 Mario already had a decade of special treatment behind him. His mother says it was almost as if he were "born with skates attached." His coaches say that at six he had the "unexplainable" gifts of anticipation and vision, which set him above all rivals except the ineffable Gretzky.

But such gifts can be a burden unless matched in the boy's character by the ability to work hard and a single-mindedness that insulates him from the jealousy, envy and abuse that are the lot of all minor hockey sensations. And one more thing: these qualities must turn up in a family where the game is honored, where parents are willing to allow their boy to give over his childhood to hockey.

Obviously the odds are against these talents and opportunities converging in one child. In the history of the game there have only been a handful of superstars who have arrived at the pantheon where Mario Lemieux now stands.

But where is he headed?

Now entering his middle twenties, the young man reiterates again and again, he does not aspire to be Wayne Gretzky; he wants to be Mario Lemieux.

What that means remains an open question. Neither the Lemieux talent nor character have yet been fully explored. Mario, "the Gentle Giant," "the Black Knight," the "Magnificent," can still become whatever he chooses — in hockey, in business, maybe even in professional golf. Aside from his outstanding physical talents, he's mature and wise in the ways of the world far beyond what you'd expect of a 23-year-old with a grade-10 education. Hitherto his life has been supremely unordinary. The rest will, no doubt, follow that pattern.

The story of Mario Lemieux begins close to the heart of Montreal, in the working-class neighborhood of Ville Emard. In 10 minutes a hockey fan could walk from the Lemieux duplex on Rue Jorgue to the fabled Montreal Forum. And Jean-Guy Lemieux, Mario's father, was just such a fan. *"Un fou de hockey,"* says his wife, Pierrette.

She remembers her honeymoon was scarcely over — she and Jean-Guy were still settling into her mother-in-law's downstairs flat — when she first felt the hypnotic power hockey was to have in her life.

Money was tight. At 18 Jean-Guy had come to the city from the farm and worked in a series of manual jobs. Entertainment was a luxury. But hockey, that was a necessity. Jean-Guy's enthusiasm for the game was far from casual. At the end of the week he always found enough to pay for their hockey tickets.

When the NHL was a six-team league Jean-Guy was a regular at the Forum. On the farm he'd never played himself. There was little opportunity and he'd had health problems. First allergies and then a peculiar lung disorder that kept him in hospital for nearly two years in his early teens.

Now as a young man in Montreal he was finally able to fully indulge his passion. In a dozen years as a spectator he watched the hometown Canadiens win the Stanley Cup an incredible seven times. In those glory years, the Lemieuxs were far from the only Montreal family to have hockey as the most significant cultural icon in their lives.

But in 1967 when Alain, the eldest of his three sons, was just six and starting to play in organized hockey, the National Hockey League, under Clarence Campbell, made a business decision that upset Jean-Guy's world. Expansion meant the well-defined rivalries of the six-team league were suddenly obscured in a 12-team roster. Three years later when the league expanded again to 14 teams, Jean-Guy dropped his season tickets and turned his attention to the considerable waves nine-year-old Alain was making in minor hockey.

There was enough to do as a hockey father. Jean-Guy understood the game and recognized kindred souls in first Alain, and then his younger two, Richard, five, and Mario, 16 months younger and only three.

Even Pierrette joined in on the family passion. In their neat little duplex there was no huge expanse of basement for her youngsters to practice. The boys were too young for shinny on the outdoor rink behind the church. And the road and even the lane beside the house had too much traffic. It seemed her impatient, boisterous crew would have to wait a bit to play hockey.

But then she had a sudden flash. In the winter she often sprinkled new snow on her carpet to freshen it. Why not really pack the snow on the rug and give the boys a place to skate?

Jean-Guy helped her carry in the snow and lace up the borrowed skates. "They were so young they were skating more on the boots than on the blades," she says through an interpreter. "But it was fun; I would have played too if I could have. All I could do was play goal."

Half-a-dozen times over the next couple of years the Lemieux living room

was transformed into an indoor hockey rink. "We still have the same rug," says Pierrette proudly, pointing down at a scarlet rug that shows no signs of wear or damage.

But the boys soon outgrew the living room. "Every day after school we used to play on the rink behind the church," says Richard, now at 25 a deliveryman for O'Keefe Brewery. "We were always together. Five or six hours every day. We'd come in for dinner and go back out again until nine or 10 at night."

The church, St. Jean de Matha, is visible from the Lemieuxs' kitchen window. The rink was no more than 300 yards from their back door.

By the time he was six Mario was also playing organized hockey, following in the footsteps of his two older brothers. Alain went through minor hockey as an outstanding player. Richard was often selected as the best defenceman. But it was the youngest, the hotshot Mario, who stood Montreal minor hockey on its ear.

At six he was the dominant player on the ice. He was a little bigger than average, but already it was his hands and hockey sense that made him exceptional. The size and strength would come later. Wherever he went there was a hubbub of equal parts jealousy and adoration around the little player who wore No. 27 in honor of his brother Alain. Pierrette and Jean-Guy watched their youngest carefully but made no move to push him up a level to play with Richard.

Every year Mario was the scoring champion and usually the MVP, as well. The very first team he played on won the Montreal championship, a feat that would be repeated in the future by most of his teams; and the glory got greater at the peewee level when his team, as city champions and so entitled to meet the champions of Quebec's nine other regions, went on to win the provincial title.

But such outlandish success had a price. Mario learned early how to deal with the fury and abuse from the losing team. Before he was 10 he could tune out jealous barbs as though they'd never been spoken. All kinds of people he didn't even know resented the little phenom from the Ville Emard Hurricanes.

But adversity even then only strengthened his resolve. He learned to be a little wary of strangers, but for the rest he shrugged it off. Inside his tight-knit, hockey-saturated family he was already a star. Perhaps a slightly coddled star, as the youngest and the most outrageously talented of the three boys.

The talent was already melded to the character it takes to be a superstar. He was five years younger than Alain but he couldn't stand losing to his older brothers. "If Mario lost, it would be as if a hurricane went through the basement," Jean-Guy told *Sports Illustrated*.

"He had his little character. It had to go his way," says Albert Mandanici, who was a scout for Pittsburgh and has watched Mario since he was six years old and played with his own son. "As Mario grew he matured into the player you see now. But he always had those hands and that hockey sense. It's a gift of God."

And if things didn't work out Mario was always inventive in getting his way. When he was eight and a babysitter refused to change the channel from a movie she was watching so he could see *Hockey Night in Canada*, he and his brothers locked her in the bathroom for the evening. To drown out her protests, they just turned up the sound.

Today that's one of the touchstone stories the family enjoys when visitors drop in for a sandwich and a beer. In the "Hall of Fame" living room on Rue Jorgue there's no escaping the subject of hockey greatness. Pierrette has decorated every square inch with trophies, sweaters and pictures of the Lemieux hockey successes. On the back of the door in from the front hall is a life-size cutout of Mario in full Pittsburgh regalia. On skates he's six-foot seven and

one-half inches, and his picture pasted on a small floral print background dominates the room just as his success dominates their lives.

"It was a good life," says Pierrette. "There was never failure, always success, always glory." Mario has offered to buy his parents a new home but they're reluctant to leave. Here on Rue Jorgue the extended family is close at hand and so are the memories. "The baptism parties for all three boys were held in the basement of this house," says Pierrette with a touch of wistfulness.

When Mario signed his first pro contract, 190 people crowded into the house, spilling over into the yard and laneway. And last year again when he won the Hart Trophy as league MVP, another wall-to-wall crowd squeezed into the six-room flat. In this cozy, hockey-consecrated living room, the Lemieux clan gathers for the Pittsburgh games. In the first years, 1984-85, there were often 30 or more people — cousins, aunts, uncles, former coaches and friends — eating Pierrette's popcorn and sandwiches and paying for the beer by buying the "50-50" tickets Pierrette sold. But the Lemieuxs didn't need to collect for the satellite dish that made the parties possible. The dish, installed on the roof, was one of the things Mario wrote into his first contract with Pittsburgh. Even if he was leaving the fold he wanted to make sure his family could see his games.

Four years later the gatherings are still going on, but only about a dozen stalwarts show up for all 74 or so televised regular-season games. The novelty has worn off, but the family is still having fun. With a smaller crowd it's a lot easier to see the game, and of course with the dramatically improved team, there's a lot more to cheer about.

Pierrette, the most lively and outgoing of the Lemieux family, sighs when she thinks of all the fun they've had with hockey. "We don't care about the jet-set life, the snobby, high people," she says, partially in English. "We wouldn't be comfortable."

But for her superstar son the choices aren't quite so simple. It's a long road from Ville Emard, Quebec, to Mount Lebanon, Pennsylvania, where Mario and his Ville Emard girlfriend, Nathalie Asselin 23, have just moved into a "16- or 18-room palace. I don't know how big it is. The rooms go on forever," says Pierrette.

But although there are many changes in the Pittsburgh Mario with his 1000-bottle wine cellar, his diamond rings and Cadillac Allante, to his family and few close friends he is still just Mario. The only adjustment Pierrette has made is to buy a slightly fancier wine when her superstar comes to dinner. "I'm happy with the $6.95 Oiseau Bleu we always had, but he says 'It won't do anymore, Mom."

The family believes Mario's heart is still in the family, still in Montreal, and still in hockey. They laugh at the prophets of doom who pronounce that Mario is changing, forgetting his old friends and becoming unduly attached to money.

The family has been through this before. All his life, every time Mario

13

moved up a division the naysayers predicted ruin. "Oh, sure, he's fine in (no contact) atom, but just wait until he gets to peewee and takes his first hit. He'll be history," they'd say with just a hint of a gloat.

Mario always surprised everyone. And as his pro career moves into high gear no doubt he will again.

CHAPTER TWO
Superstar in the Making

*"His game hasn't really changed. He's just adjusted it
to better-quality players. I honestly believe he had
to work harder in peewee than he does in the NHL. He got
so much bigger and stronger. If you saw video of Mario
in peewee and Mario now, you'd see the same moves."*
— Ron Stevenson, retired Montreal sergeant of detectives,
Lemieux's coach from age 10 to 14

When Mario first came to peewee, the coach, Ron Stevenson, knew what was coming. The older Lemieux, Alain, had been a significant talent and everybody knew the young one coming up was even better. Stevenson had also heard the talk that Mario wouldn't survive the hitting which is first allowed in peewee. Alain certainly hadn't liked it.

So it was with curiosity and a slight sense of apprehension that he watched Mario's first game. As luck would have it they played Notre Dame de Grace, the most physical team in the league.

But even at 11, Mario had the sense of occasion that has given hockey fans some of their greatest thrills in the past few years. And then, as now, he thrived on confounding his critics. Stevenson still shakes his head in wonder as he recalls that first game. "The NDG Maroons were tough and hit hard, but they couldn't even touch him. He got eight goals."

Gradually Mario fell under the tutelage of Stevenson, who was renowned as a tough, demanding and very successful coach. He was a sergeant of detectives for the Montreal Police Department, and his cronies would often come and watch the budding superstar. While many of the other boys on the team, as they watched Stevenson, thought police work might be a good career, Mario never wavered; he wanted to play in the NHL.

Stevenson coached Mario for four of the most impressionable years of his life — from 10 to 14 right through to the end of his Bantam years. And every year but the first they won the provincial championship.

Mario remembers his coach as the man who taught him to respect others. Stevenson remembers how he drilled work habits and self-discipline into all his young, very talented charges.

Mario wasn't the only hotshot on the team. Jean-Jacques Daigneault and

Marc Bergevin, both NHL players now, were the class of the team when Mario arrived. They were both a year older and Stevenson remembers that for all Mario's phenom status and "charisma" on the ice, Daigneault wasn't "that far behind. All three were outstanding." In that first year the older boys set the pace for excellence.

Meanwhile, at the Forum and on their TV screens, the kids of the Ville Emard Hurricanes were watching Guy Lafleur make history. This was 1977-78. Le Demon Blond was in full flight. The year before, en route to the Stanley Cup, he'd made history with 56 goals and 80 assists, the best season any Montreal Canadien has ever had. And in French Canada the Lafleur legend was already very strong. Everyone knew the stories of Guy's early-morning excursions to the rink in Thurso to practice alone before going to school. The story was a powerful incantation to youngsters like Mario, intent on following in his skate strides.

Certainly Coach Stevenson had no trouble getting them to practice. "They were on the ice five days out of seven," he remembers. "They usually played three games a week, but when they weren't playing they'd practice. Mario and his two linemates, Stephane Lepage on left wing and Sylvain Cote on right, would pass the puck around like it was on a string," says Stevenson. "They'd practice the same drill over and over. If they were passing left, the boy on the right would skate for hours and never even touch the puck. They were very serious about hockey.

"I always made them work very, very hard physically in practice. They didn't know any other way to play."

In the games the intensity of the practice showed. Stevenson once asked Mario how he'd known who he was passing to when he dropped the puck behind him. "I could tell it was Stephane by the sound of his skates," Mario replied.

Stevenson never remembers Mario missing a practice or a game in four years. One morning his mother called to say Mario was ill, but when Stevenson arrived at the rink that afternoon the boy was already in the dressing room lacing up his skates.

"I had to bring him," Pierrette later explained. "He was breaking up the house."

Such displays of emotion were usually confined to the Lemieux home. Stevenson remembers how quiet Mario was getting ready for a game. He'd make a point of saying hello to each of his teammates but then he'd sit in the corner and not say another word until they hit the ice. For the big games he often asked the coach for a lift to the arena. "He'd sit in the back seat and you couldn't get a word out of him," Stevenson remembers.

Self-discipline was an important part of Stevenson's system, but when it failed the coach was there to rekindle the flame. He rarely checked curfews, expecting his players to monitor themselves. However, when he ran into a flagrant breach

of the rules, he didn't hesitate to lower the boom.

In Mario's final year of bantam, several of the players missed curfew on the Friday night of a big tournament in Chicoutimi. Stevenson ordered the whole team to bed at 7:30 p.m. on the Saturday night. "The players complained afterward about how hard it was to get to sleep," Stevenson says with a chuckle. "They hadn't been to bed that early since they were six. But Mario came out the next day with a big, big game. He scored 11 points — eight goals and three assists."

If they made mistakes in the game, Stevenson was equally fierce. A hundred or more lines was the normal consequence of taking a bad penalty. Mario got no special treatment.

But even in writing lines he had a mind of his own. "I'd tell him to write 'I must not take bad penalties' 100 times," says Stevenson, "but he'd add his own ideas. There'd be one line of 'I must not take bad penalties' but the next would be 'I must work harder on back-checking,' or 'I must improve my shot.'"

Stevenson recognized Mario's hard headedness even then. "It's probably one of the things that makes him so great," he says. "He really believes in himself.

And if he doesn't like somebody like Dave King (coach of the Canadian national team) he'll never want anything to do with him. No matter what."

But in four years Stevenson saw no evidence that Mario was in any way the "coach killer" he was later labeled. "In four years I never had any trouble with him at all. My reward for 30 years of coaching hockey was the opportunity to coach Mario Lemieux. He was a great boy, as well as an outstanding player."

Mario was captain in his second year with Stevenson and always showed maturity and responsibility in that position. When he was 12, Greg Choutes, a hot new prospect from Point St. Charles, came to play with the Hurricanes. But the integration process wasn't working out. Stevenson was afraid the boy was going to quit the team.

"Do you want him to play with us?" Mario asked his coach. "Then fix it up that he stays with me this weekend."

"He wanted to win so badly," recalls Stevenson, "that rather than stay with his friends for the weekend and have fun at the tournament, he'd spend the time helping a new youngster get used to the team. The two of them ended up good friends. Choutes was very good but he stopped growing. He ended up in the American League, and eventually went back to university."

There were other signs of Mario's burgeoning maturity. He still hated to lose, but there would be no emotional displays afterward in the dressing room. He would be very, very quiet and withdrawn, nothing more. "You knew he was unhappy but he didn't say anything," says Stevenson.

As they moved up through bantam and the cheap shots and physical abuse got nastier and more determined, Stevenson watched his star struggle to keep his cool. "Once in a while I'd have to calm him down. I'd tell him to get control of himself and have him miss a couple of shifts. Just like now, it was the opposition's game plan to get him off his game."

Mario could see very clearly that by losing control he was bowing to his opponents, and that, in his lexicon of behavior, was forbidden. He was also being told by a man who'd never led him wrong that it would do his career good if he showed more respect to people both on and off the ice.

To live with these two dicta he was going to have to show a forbearance that required almost saintly discipline from a youngster just hitting puberty. A youngster whose strength and size were beginning to catch up with his head.

But Mario recognized his coach's wisdom. In later years he'd tell Bill Houston of the *Globe and Mail:* "I always liked him (Stevenson). He was the kind of guy who taught me a lot of things when I was young. They were just little things. For one, 'You tend to be impolite with people.'

"He wanted me to be polite with the older people, with the parents and people surrounding me. He said you should respect others and I think I learned that."

Most of the time he carried it off, Stevenson now marvels. And if he's with-

drawn and "leery of strangers" on occasion, it's little wonder. He learned early to expect anything.

"On at least two occasions mothers of the opposing teams spat in his face," says Stevenson. "He'd want to stay and watch Alain play after our game, but if he went for a soft drink I'd have to send three or four of our players with him for protection."

When he was 12, the Hurricanes played a tournament in Ottawa in which Mario had one of his "Mario-type games," scoring 12 points. Afterward a writer from the *Ottawa Citizen* wanted to interview Mario and take his picture.

"I couldn't let him," recalls Stevenson. "Mario was in the shower when I went to find him. With just a towel around him, he looked like a beaten child. He had two black eyes, which didn't help either, but there were slashes and marks all over his body. It was brutal."

By the time he got into bantam, Mario hit his first growth spurt, and he was harder to hit because of his new size and speed. He'd always been a little bigger than average, but now the final ace up his hockey sleeve started to kick into place. By 16 he would be six-foot four and weigh 200 pounds.

Over the summer before bantam, his teammates and coach watched their star begin to shoot up in height, and they smiled secretly. Mario had already begun to learn how to give back what he got when the ref wasn't watching and how to protect himself. Now with the beginnings of his "pterodactyl reach" starting to show, the scales would be more balanced. As Stevenson says, hockey would never be as tough again for Mario as it was in peewee.

But growing brought its own set of problems. As Pierrette had always known about all of her brood, they needed their sleep. After a tough game she'd always let Mario sleep in the next morning. Coach Stevenson was always after him to make sure he got enough rest. Now it was even more important.

In Pittsburgh several of Lemieux's roommates on the road have complained that the superstar never does anything *but* sleep. Journalists make cracks about the 12 hours a night he is rumored to prefer. But Stevenson and Mario's brother Richard are indignant about the criticisms.

"Sports takes a lot of energy," says Richard. "And Mario plays 30 or 35 minutes a game."

Stevenson, who expected Mario to carry the team many nights, wanted him to sleep as much as he could. He was big and he was growing bigger. He probably used up more energy just lugging around the extra weight, Stevenson reasoned. Besides, nobody can estimate what psychic toll both the abuse and the attention exacted from a boy who was essentially shy and reserved.

Certainly then as now Mario often needed to withdraw and be alone. Perhaps it's that process that allows him to provide the explosions of magic that have always characterized his game.

And when the season was over and Mario had won the obligatory scoring championship and the team had triumphed in the province, the Hurricane organization wanted the boys to forget about hockey. It was a grueling year, often running to 75 games, and they needed a break. Summer hockey schools and clinics were actively discouraged.

Mario was delighted. As much as he loved the game, summer was a time to be outside, a time for . . . baseball. Here again he excelled. When he was 12 and 13, people remember watching him pitch no-hitters with the same lackadaisical ease he now displays when stuffing the puck in the net.

But the baseball and hockey seasons overlapped a bit. And one thing Mario never had was the fecundity of physical vitality some athletes demonstrate. Even now after 12 hours' sleep, he doesn't bounce back from extreme exertion the way Gretzky, five and a half years older, does.

So as he started to grow taller, using a lot of energy in the process, it became clear he would have to settle for one sport. In Ville Emard hockey was the obvious choice, especially since it was by then clear to anyone with eyes that Mario Lemieux, if he continued as he was, would one day be a dominant player in the NHL.

Was his a charmed childhood? Well, clearly it was a preparation for a life that bears little similarity to most. When he was 11, and named Player of the Month in Montreal minor hockey, he was honored equally with his hero — Guy Lafleur, the Montreal Canadien Player of the Month. That picture is the kind of keepsake very few of us ever get.

It also imposes expectations few of us ever feel.

When Mario was 12, former great Yvan Cournoyer saw him play and insisted that Scotty Bowman come to a Hurricane game. A couple of days later Bowman was quoted in the press: "We're running all over the world looking for talent, and last week, in our own back yard, I saw the best prospect I've ever seen."

There's no record of how such a statement from the wizard of the Canadiens affected the 12-year-old schoolboy.

But somewhere in the Montreal suburb of Ste. Julie, Bob Perno, hockey agent Gus Badali's Quebec lieutenant, tucked those words away in the back of his mind for future reference. When the seed flowered a few years later it would mean that Mario would spend time with and get advice from another Badali client, Wayne Gretzky.

There were other remarkable moments that must have left their mark on an impressionable boy. When Lafleur scored his five hundredth goal, Mario was sitting right behind the Canadiens' bench in the Forum. One of Pierrette's prized possessions is the newspaper photo showing Guy's elation and in the background her own boy's shy enigmatic smile.

The grooming for greatness went on in both the little things and the big. At

15 Mario spent two weeks at Berlitz getting ready to deal with the inevitable onslaught from the English media.

And at his regular school it was acknowledged his priorities lay elsewhere. If he slept in or missed a day, very little was said. He sailed along in the middle of the pack, and neither parents nor teachers asked for more. Even the local priest understood Mario was the hockey player.

At home when Mario wanted something he got it. And if Mario made a decision, his family backed him to the hilt. His older brother Richard, who'd quit hockey at 15, would carry his equipment out after the games. No embarrassment, no resentment; just quiet pride in his brother's wondrous achievements.

The family knew better than anyone how much this "charmed childhood" had cost and burdened the boy. And they were determined to ease his way, however they could, to his ultimate goal: to be the best in the world.

CHAPTER THREE
Setting a Course

"We knew an exceptional was coming."
— Pierre Lacroix, agent for much of the cream
of Quebecois hockey players

It's a a long haul from bantam to the NHL — even for a perennial MVP who's played on half-a-dozen provincial championship teams. Mario at 14 knew he still had a number of corners to negotiate before he could make good on the promise Scotty Bowman had seen in him.

Of course he was supremely well-positioned to do it. He'd won every award on the table, and when he moved on to Montreal Midget Triple A he moved into a world already agog over his talent.

But the boy who had always been shy and retiring now became really withdrawn. Within the family fold he was the same Mario, but to strangers who met him for the first time he seemed remote, set apart from his team and everybody else by his immense talent.

The team was not particularly blessed in talent except for their star center, but Mario still broke a midget scoring record with 62 goals. Every move he made that season — 1980-81 — was carefully weighed and recorded by the host of junior scouts hanging around.

It was already clear to everyone Mario was the best of the crop, but were there any other late bloomers who might give him incentive to work harder? With his new size and strength it all looked so unspeakably easy for the string bean still wearing No. 27 in honor of his older brother.

But nobody came within striking distance, and when the junior draft was held in May, Mario as number-one pick was shuffled off to the last-place Laval Voisins, where there hadn't been much to cheer about since Mike Bossy had sparkled in 1977 when the team was still called the Nationals. Everything was going according to plan — except that he was going to have to leave home. This would be the hard part.

But he needed a little toughening. The year he'd just been through, things had gone on in the pro ranks that must have struck at the heart of the young Lemieux. People who met him after this year were struck by his maturity, by the way he knew exactly what he wanted. They shouldn't have been, for 1980-81 was an incubation year, a great object lesson for the youngster with the brushcut who, until then, thought only of playing for his hometown team.

"I think every kid who grows up in Montreal wants to play for the Canadiens, and I was no different," he told *Maclean's* early in 1989. "Lafleur was the best player in the world when I was growing up and he was certainly my idol."

But idols can have horrific years. And 1980-81 was the beginning of the first ending for Guy Lafleur. The start was the sensational headlines after the fire in the guest house of his Baie d'Urfe home. The season ended on the operating table where he had the top of his ear reconstructed after coming a hair's breadth from being decapitated in a car accident.

But it was the horror show on the ice that must have given Mario greater pause. For, that year he appeared to have lost his touch. He could still skate like the wind, but when he got to the net he was suddenly awkward. He didn't appear to know how to maneuver the little piece of black rubber past the defender in goal. He fumbled, bobbled and often mistimed his shot, or didn't shoot at all.

He was injured seven times and was off for nine extended periods. He was only 29. Was it over already?

The worst part for Lafleur fans — and Mario certainly was one — was the way Montreal management and the press were sniping at him. Here was the man who had handed them four Stanley Cups being berated and chastised like a mere mortal.

To Mario the lesson was clear. It would take Guy with his different, more trusting nature longer to figure it out. A hockey player, even a magnificent superstar, must look out for himself. No one else can, or will, do it for him.

The second lesson was drawn from the humiliation of Doug Wickenheiser. Mario, of course, with his rough ride through minor hockey could be under no illusion that hockey fans were a gentle lot. But the merciless treatment Wickenheiser got in Montreal was startling in its cruelty.

Wickenheiser was picked number one overall, just as Mario dreamed of being one day. But the success turned to ash in his mouth before he'd played a month of his first NHL season. Before he'd even got used to his new team uniform he was riding the bench and being proclaimed as a major disappointment, and more importantly a major mistake.

He never did — never could — live up to expectations. To the fans and media, Wickenheiser was always the bum Montreal GM Irving Grundman and recruitment chief Ron Caron perversely chose over Denis Savard. He was never forgiven for their folly.

Like Guy, Wickenheiser was visibly shaken. The youngster who had reigned supreme in Regina when he played for the Pats, had been cocky, outgoing, and a natural leader. Now he was bottled up at the end of the bench getting next to no ice time and plenty of abuse.

Like Guy he was cultivating a reputation as a Crescent Street partyer. It certainly was more fun than playing hockey under those trying conditions.

How would Mario fare under such a microscope? Subjected to daily second-guessing in the press and the apparently arbitrary whims of Claude Ruel, who was already trying to orient the Canadiens' style to more defensive play than Forum fans were used to seeing.

No wonder Mario would soon tell whoever asked he didn't want to play in Montreal. "Too much pressure," he'd say.

Today his brother Richard reiterates the family's sentiments from those days. "Wickenheiser was a really nice guy. Look what happened to him."

(In the 1988-89 season Wickenheiser played with an AHL team, Team Canada and was finally called up to the Washington Capitals late in the season. He has never in nine years up and down in the NHL really caught on with any team. His confidence was badly shaken by the Montreal experience and he turned himself into a defensive player, never again recovering his winning touch with the puck.)

By this time a family style was developing around Mario. He was the youngest, but nobody told him what to do. He watched, asked various people for advice, thrashed out a decision and stuck to it. His family, who knew how seriously he 27

thought about everything, backed him to the hilt. Never did they try to alter his decisions once they were made. If Mario thought it was best to leave Montreal for more money and less pressure south of the border, it was. No question.

This was the 15-year-old (two months shy of 16) Bob Perno met at a hockey-evaluation clinic at the University of Montreal in August, 1981. In his files of potential clients he still had the clipping of three years ago. Bowman had never seen a better prospect, eh? Perno would see.

Yes, he would see. "When I saw him on ice I had flashes of Wayne Gretzky," Perno remembers. He saw everything Bowman had seen, as well as two new ingredients — size and assurance. Lemieux, not quite 16, was already approaching six feet and already very much "his own man."

Perno was excited. "We (Perno and his boss, Gus Badali) had represented Wayne Gretzky in junior. I knew Mario was going to have that kind of impact."

He shrugged off the scuttlebutt in the stands. "Swelled-headed, lazy, self-centered" were the most common adjectives for the lanky No. 27, who toyed with the puck and the other players like a cat with a mouse.

"When I met him that night with his family, he was none of those things. Through the first five years (of working with Mario) I never thought of him as arrogant or self-centered. He was easy to handle and like a member of the

family. He used to sleep on that couch," says Perno, pointing to the sofa in his office.

Things have changed, and Perno and Badali have been replaced by a big-time Pittsburgh baseball agent named Tom Reich (pronounced Rich). Perno smarts under the change because they'd been such good friends. "There are so many stories," he says wistfully.

Lemieux's shirt from his first year in Pittsburgh hangs just inside the door to Perno's office. The fat scrapbook on the coffee table is crammed with the highlights of Lemieux's junior career and entry into the NHL.

But none of that could be glimpsed on that first August night when Perno went back with Lemieux to Rue Jorgue to talk business. Right from the beginning Perno found Lemieux "streetsmart."

"That's a tough neighborhood he grew up in," Perno explains. "He seemed like a kid. He still does, but inside the wheels are always turning. You can't put anything over on that guy."

Perno's assessment is full of respect. He was astonished at the maturity of the young phenom. That night he promised that if Mario kept up the pace, broke all the records in junior it seemed he was poised to break, and if he was number-one pick in the 1984 draft, they would get him a certain figure in his first contract. A figure Perno says now, without divulging the exact amount, that was higher than any rookie contract in the history of the game.

"Of course there were other agents pursuing him but I think he chose us because we represented Gretzky. Wayne was becoming his hero."

By 1981 it was painfully obvious the torch had been passed from Lafleur to Gretzky. In February, with only 56 points, Lafleur quipped that he would need "about 10 points a game for the last 18 games to win the scoring title, and even if I did that Gretzky would probably get 11."

Gretzky finished the season with a then NHL record of 164 points and won the Hart Trophy as the league's most valuable player. Yes, Mario thought, he would like to meet him.

Perno and his big solemn client took the train to Toronto. "Wayne was so gracious. He sat down with him and gave him advice about handling the media pressure, about girls, and even about discipline. It was great."

A few weeks later they were back again. This time to golf in Badali's golf tournament. It was one of the first times Mario had played golf and he was already showing signs of immense talent in this sport, too.

Perno remembers Mario's great belief in his own ability. He wasn't boastful, just unshakably confident. On the way back from the tournament Perno mulled over the exceptional qualities of the young man slumped beside him. How could they draw attention to them?

Was there some number he could wear that would underline his promise? Mario himself was content to keep his brother's number. It certainly had served him well. Perno was looking for something with more meaning.

"What about 99? Wayne's my idol," Mario suggested.

Too presumptuous, Perno thought. Besides, it would cause the young player to face an incredible load of expectation. "I told him he needed a distinctive number that would bring attention but that no one else was wearing."

Perno suggested No. 66. It would, of course, invite the obvious comparison, but it wouldn't tread on The Great One's toes. Yes, Mario agreed, it was just the ticket.

With a number chosen and a team that needed him, the stage was set for the most remarkable career in the annals of Quebec junior hockey. Laval Voisin coach Jean Begin was looking forward to the 1981-82 season and coaching the gangly 16-year-old who was already one of the most outstanding players in the country.

When Lemieux signed his contract — for an undisclosed amount — he promised Voisin owner, Claude Fornel, that the team would win the Memorial Cup at some point in his junior career. This was no idle boast. Mario believed absolutely he could make it happen.

He didn't — and doesn't — make promises lightly. Fornel, he said, could count on him. Begin rejoiced at the prospect of such a dramatic turnaround.

But Mario, alone and lonely in a Laval boardinghouse, did not immediately pick up the pulses of the Laval fans. In his first year in the league, he got a mere 30 goals and 66 assists for what was described as a "paltry" total in the high-scoring QMJHL (Quebec Major Junior Hockey League) of 96 points.

He was too tired and there was too much pressure, explains his brother Richard. During the summer of 1982 he decided it was time to pinpoint his focus. Although he was just shy of 17 he explained to his father he planned to quit school. The year before he'd only got to class a day or two a week, but the expectations burdened him. He wanted to have his mind clear so he could skate in the morning and not be too tired to play at night. If it didn't work out in the NHL, he said, he could always go back to school.

As with most of Mario's decisions this one showed wisdom. His point production immediately almost doubled. He finished the year with 184 points — 84 goals and 100 assists.

He suspects the number might have been higher except for the detour he took to play from the Canadian team in the World Junior Championships in Moscow. That was a disastrous series for Mario. After the first three games — where he didn't see much ice time playing center on the fourth line — he was benched completely.

Some would have had their belief in themselves shaken by such disregard, but not Mario. He came back incensed, outraged, insulted. It didn't help when Canadian-team Coach Dave King, questioned about his use of Lemieux, told the

national media he had been put on the fourth line after training camp because of a committee vote by five people. In the Montreal dailies the explanation was that he was too slow on his skates.

Not surprisingly Mario wondered why he had subjected himself to this, and he vowed never to do it again. There were other problems. He came back mentally fatigued, and the Voisins, in first place when he'd left, had gone into a tailspin. He wasn't able to get them going again.

His personal statistics were similarly affected. When he'd left for Russia he had been the scoring leader, but Pat LaFontaine took over in his absence and he never recovered the lead. The young superstar felt the whole debacle was his fault. He'd let his team down. He was getting his first taste of defeat.

But people who make it to the front rank in any walk of life are not the kind who repeat mistakes. He promised Fornel it wouldn't happen again. And although the price turned out to be incalcuably higher than he expected, it didn't.

The fringe benefits
to the job, a stylish
diamond ring.

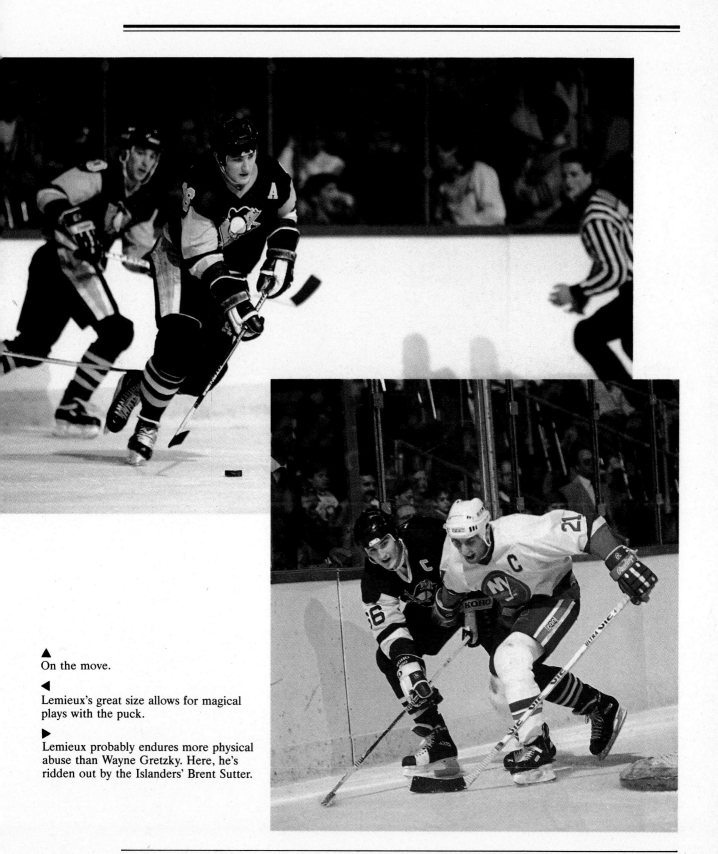

▲
On the move.

◄
Lemieux's great size allows for magical plays with the puck.

►
Lemieux probably endures more physical abuse than Wayne Gretzky. Here, he's ridden out by the Islanders' Brent Sutter.

▲
A family portrait and celebration of excellence.

◄
Lemieux was named to the NHL all-star team for the Rendez-Vous '87 Series against the Soviet Union.

Another year, another banquet, more awards. ▲

▶
It was during Canada Cup '87 that Lemieux finally silenced his detractors.

▲
Lemieux uses his extraordinary reach to score another goal.

▶
In the spotlight — again.

▶
Lemieux never allows traffic to keep him from the puck.

▲
Lemieux has a passion for golf in the off-season.

◄
A shooting star.

▲
Ready for another shift.

▶
Looking for action.

◀

At the annual NHL all-star game.

▼

On the move at the 1989 all-star game in Edmonton.

Getting ready for
a Rendez-Vous
with the Soviets.

Canada Cup '87
brought out the
best in Lemieux.

Holding the silverware.

CHAPTER FOUR
Draft Year

"I'd trade all 12 picks for him."
— Lou Nanne, GM of the Minnesota North Stars in 1984

I n a young hockey player's life nothing quite matches the *Sturm und Drang* of the year he turns 18. Everything he's done before fades into insignificance compared to his draft-year statistics. If he's to grow, this is the year to do it. If he's to have one brilliant kick at the scoring-title can, this is it. If he's to shine in battle as a tough guy, this is the year to wreak the havoc. And if he's to have one colossal binge of mental toughness the larger-than-life tension of draft year is the platform on which to strut his stuff.

Consider the case of the young Mario. Since peewee the weight of expectations had been exorbitant. Now it approached the impossible.

In some ways he'd designed his own pressure cooker. He'd made two grandiose promises: first, to deliver to Mr. Fornel Le Coupe Memorial; second, to his agents, to break all the records and make himself the number-one draft choice in the world.

Quite a high-wire act for an 18-year-old. Throughout the crises of his draft year he was a raw teenager standing up alone to a country's wrath, and resisting the entire hierarchy of a game that had made him what he was, and now claimed he was putting himself ahead of the game and everyone connected with it.

The seeds of the problem with patriotism were found in the 1983 World Junior Championships. After the debacle in Russia he decided not to participate again. There were three reasons, says Perno, who stood by while the screws were tightened on his star client. First, Mario had been insulted by his treatment in 1983. Second, he felt he needed the two games he would miss if he had any hope of breaking Guy Lafleur's 1970-71 scoring record of 130 goals. And third, he worried about tiring himself and missing games that might help him reach his goal of winning the Memorial Cup as a Laval Voisin. (Though, in mid-November when the storm clouds were gathering, Laval looked a shoo-in with a 20-3-2 record. Lemieux already had 101 points in 25 games.)

"I've been thinking about my decision for a long time," he told the press in early December, 1983, "ever since we came back from the tournament last year. It was very tough to play in the league after. I was tired. It hurt my game."

So when the Canadian hockey establishment invited him to represent his

country in the tournament in Sweden, he refused. It would not be the same coach, they pointed out. He would not have to play on the fourth line, they promised. But Mario was adamant. The tournament began Christmas Day. On that day he would be home in Ville Emard with his family, he said.

They cajoled. They demanded. And when he was steadfast in his refusal, they tried bullying. The QMJHL suspended him for 10 days; with the suspension he would miss the same three games he would miss if he played in the World Junior tournament.

He answered that challenge with lawyer André Champagne in the Quebec Superior Court. On December 28, 1983, he applied for an injunction. His contractual obligation was only to the Laval Voisins, Champagne argued; his client was not obliged to play for Team Canada. The judge agreed and Lemieux was reinstated.

Still the patriots vilified him. "What is happening bothers me," he told reporters as his point production dwindled to two and a half a game, "but I'm trying to concentrate on my game. I don't want to think about it, or what people say about me in the papers."

He weathered the controversy, but in February when Jacques Olivier was settling into his new portfolio as the minister of sports, he muddied the waters again by bringing up Lemieux's name and saying he might have played for Team Canada had there been a French-speaking coach.

"Some people have told me that he (Lemieux) refused to play because he had a lot of trouble with (head coach Dave) King. Mr. King is a very good man, but maybe there was a misunderstanding between an Anglophone and a Francophone. Unfortunately we lost a very great athlete."

Nonsense, says Perno now, but at the time it seemed Mario couldn't escape getting pulled deeper into the vortex of controversy. His image was sullied and his play affected. The vultures were poised for the feast.

First up the Montreal Canadiens. Mario had several reasons not to want to play for the hometown Canadiens: Wickenheiser's humiliation; Lafleur's struggle with the new defensive regime; and the new Liberal party tax laws, which made it more lucrative to play south of the border. Mario didn't hesitate to let his preference be known.

"I think it will be better for me to go to the United States," he said in April, 1984. "I'm not so known and there won't be so much expectation. I think it will be better for my career."

Montreal, in its usual fashion, had maneuvered to get the first-round pick of the lowly Hartford Whalers. They expected to pick third, fourth or fifth. As Mario's statistics improved and he seemed on course to break every record in the book, his numbers "were monitored like Hank Aaron's were when Aaron closed in on Babe Ruth's all-time home-run record," enthused *USA Today*.

But in the executive suite of the Montreal Forum there was no such enthu-

siasm. "Lemieux is just one of the premium players we're looking at," huffed GM Serge Savard in January. In March he added he wasn't sure if Lemieux would make it in the pros. "I keep wondering about him. I've seen him in six road games and he hasn't done a thing. The next night he scores a bunch of goals. I don't know about him. I really don't."

Others, who wouldn't allow their names to be used, were calling Lemieux "lazy," "chippy," and worse.

Had Mario been more like Guy Lafleur and inclined to doubt himself the tactics might have made inroads. But unswervable confidence had marked Mario from the beginning. This was a glory year and the Lemieux gravy train would roll over the niggling problems.

He would finish the season with 14 league records and 23 team records. Every game was a sellout. People came from miles to see the junior sensation. Guy Lafleur remembers seeing him on two different occasions. "I think he got three or four goals each time," he says with a laugh.

Mario continued to be the great occasion player he still is, and the greatest occasion of them all was the last game of the regular season.

He needed three goals to beat Lafleur's stunning 129-goal season in 1970-71. Mario didn't stop at three; he got six on his way to an 11-point night.

Gretzky and Oiler teammate Paul Coffey were in the stands that night for a glimpse of the future. They caught Lemieux in the corridor after it was over in what some observers remember as a wild victory dance.

In the Quebec playoffs that followed, Mario got another 29 goals in 14 games. The Voisins were on course to annihilate all comers in the Memorial Cup series, which opened the third week of May in Kitchener, Ontario.

Inexplicably the Mario magic disconnected.

People had come from all over southern Ontario to see what all the fuss was about. Fifteen or more GMs from NHL teams were huddled, prepared to envy the extraordinary luck of Eddie Johnston, the Pittsburgh honcho who would pick first.

This was the party line: barely once a decade does a talent like Lemieux come along. "You could build a franchise around him," predicted Minnesota's Lou Nanne wistfully.

And then came the pratfall.

"It was as close as he ever came to failure," remembers Perno. "I remember those nights after the games the long postmortems with his parents. I don't think Mario knew what was wrong. He'd played nearly 100 games at a super-natural pace; maybe he was just worn out."

Perno remembers the four games — Laval was the first team eliminated — as "a nightmare. Everything went wrong. It even snowed in May!"

Coach Jean Begin juggled the lines. Mario was no longer teamed with his successful partners, Jacques Goyette and Alain Brisson, but nothing could induce Mario, as Wayne Parrish, now sports editor of the *Toronto Sun* put it, to "emerge from his ennui."

Mario himself talked about being asleep at the wheel. "Maybe he just woke me up a little," he said after one game where he had suddenly come alive and scored two goals. "Sometimes I have to be woken up."

That was not a comment, true though it may have been, designed to placate the NHL brain trust. People talked of the revocation of Mario's "licence to score," of his lack of "60-minute intensity."

The "lazy" tag that had dogged even his most brilliant year now got a full workout. The assembled GMs admitted he could be incomparable but "it will be interesting to see if he has the drive that Gretzky or Lafleur have," said Barry Fraser, the Oilers' director of player personnel and considered one of the shrewder eyes for talent in the league.

The assembled GMs didn't exactly laugh behind their hands, but the green of their envy toned down a shade or two. One admitted, anonymously of course, he was glad not to be picking first and thus was spared what he imagined would be a difficult talent to integrate.

But Penguin GM, former goalie Eddie Johnston, just grinned. Let them say what they would. "Even if he stinks the joint out every night (next year), I won't change my mind," he told one writer. "He can do it in every league he plays in. I've seen him."

But while Johnston's bravado sounded hearty, he was up to his eyeballs in contract problems with the intractable Gus Badali. After every game he made a point of talking to Mario, trying to encourage him and draw him out. "He babysat him through the whole series," remembers one observer.

And three or four times during the series he sat down with Perno and Badali and tried to work out the contract. They'd certainly tried before. Three months of talking had already proved only one thing: they had very different ideas of what Mario was worth.

Today it's known that Johnston, the likable former goalie and Montreal native, wanted to sign Mario at any cost. His mission was to save the Pittsburgh franchise and Mario was his only hope. He was negotiating from the deep pockets of one of the richest men in North America — Edward DeBartolo, though the difference between $700,000 and $1-million wouldn't have dented that fabled fortune.

But billions aren't accumulated through careless negotiation, and any hockey salary creates a domino effect through the league. The negotiations were "very, very tough," Perno remembers.

Mario was deeply disappointed by his poor showing in the Memorial Cup — he scored two goals in three games — but it didn't incline him to moderate his demands. Perno had promised a certain number three years ago. That's what he wanted. Perno still smiles as he recalls Mario's persistence.

"I remember after the final game of the season, when he got 11 points," says Perno, "he stuck his head out of the dressing room and said, 'Remember what you said that night at my parents' place? I've done my job, now you do yours.'"

Perno refuses to reveal the number he had in mind. "I thought it was fair to both parties. I still do," he says now.

Negotiations dragged on over the next couple of weeks. On the eve of the June 9 draft in Montreal they were still miles apart.

Pittsburgh was behaving as though the contract had already been initialed and filed away. They'd arranged for a live feed to be linked up from the Forum to the Civic Arena in Pittsburgh. Word in Montreal was they'd already sold 8000 tickets to watch the historic drafting of Mario Lemieux.

Elaborate pamphlets offering season's tickets had been sent out. They featured a No. 66 Penguin shirt. From the text and the pictures it sounded as if Lemieux were the only player on the team.

The 18-year-old was more furious than flattered. "If they want to use me without paying me, they aren't going to get away with it," he told Perno.

"He was really steamed — I've never seen him that hot," Perno remembers. But his trusted agent wasn't the only one he sounded off to. The headline *Les Penguins ne me feront plier* (The Penguins won't make me bend) screamed in the French press on the Thursday before the Saturday draft.

The star center and his agent used the only leverage they had: they threatened not to show up at the draft.

"It's hard to negotiate when they want you for nothing and you want the big bucks," Lemieux told *Toronto Sun* hockey writer Scott Morrison in an odd moment of communicativeness.

On the night before the draft, Friday, June 8, Johnston phoned at about 9 p.m. and said he had a new offer. "Gus and I went down to the Sheraton and talked until 3 a.m.," remembers Perno. "Although we got a lot closer it was still not acceptable to Mario. The next day we thought since EJ had made the move the night before we should go to the draft. Mario's parents were very disappointed he wasn't going to go."

Mario's anger was just under the surface, but he decided "for my family and my public" to go. "We arrived 45 minutes early so if there were any last-minute negotiations we could do it in the corridor if necessary," Perno explained. Johnston and the Pittsburgh camp kept their distance until the ceremony got under way.

To no one's surprise Mario's was the first name called. He stood and waved and sat back down again. This was a contravention of one of the hallowed NHL

57

rituals. The elated draftee is supposed to make his way down to the table, shake hands, put on the team sweater, smile for the camera and generally look grateful.

"I'm no hypocrite," the 18-year-old would later explain to newsmen. "I didn't want to go down to table because the negotiations are not going well. I didn't want to put on a Pittsburgh sweater because I don't think they want me badly enough."

Although Johnston would later say this was a grandstand play by the agents, it was pure Mario. The principle was important. He does not like to be pushed. As he says, "If somebody yells at me to hurry up, I slow down. I don't like being yelled at."

And on the inside of this experience it was hard not to feel he was being pushed around. He was sitting in the Forum between Perno and his mother when his name was called. As he sat down, the media, alerted by the earlier threats, swarmed him. "He was suffocating under them," says Perno. "Then EJ called his name a second time. He got up — he had decided to go down. His mother was crying beside him. A Pittsburgh representative grabbed his arm and said, 'You have to come now.'

"Gus was right there and he said, 'Don't put any more pressure on him.' 'The Pittsburgh guy said, 'Stay out of this; it's none of your business.'"

Mario hadn't said a word, but this was too much. "Don't tell me what to do when you don't want to pay me what I'm worth," Perno remembers him hissing at the Pittsburgh emissary. As he sat down heavily, he added, "It *is* their business. I'm not going."

In the Civic Arena back in Pittsburgh, 4000 paying customers booed loudly and threw cups at the screen. In NHL cities around the continent the press trotted out the label they'd been reserving for just such a display of petulance. "Coach Killer," they called him. In the clubby circle of NHL GMs, the chortles of the envious that had begun with the poor performance in the Memorial Cup turned to loud guffaws. Eddie Johnston coming off a 16-win season was not out of the woods yet.

Al Strachan of the *Globe and Mail* wrote that Johnston should immediately get rid of the sulking ingrate. He suggested auctioning Mario off to the highest bidder, and if that didn't work maybe the Nordiques or Canadiens could be persuaded to overlook his obvious lack of character for the fan appeal of a homegrown talent.

The only place Mario's action was appreciated or understood was in the French-language Montreal dailies. They liked the idea of the French-speaking kid with the gigantic talent refusing to take whatever the English-speaking hockey establishment decided to offer. "I'm a Francophone and the draft is in Quebec and I'm not afraid to stand up to them," Mario told them. They revered him for it.

Tom Lapointe, who writes for the *Journal de Montréal* dates his friendship with Lemieux back to that crisis. "Everybody was criticizing him because he refused to wear the Penguin sweater, but he was right. I said he will be the franchise; they should treat him with respect."

Five days later the crisis was over; Mario was signed to a two-year $700,000 contract. The signing bonus was a reputed $150,000. Much was made of the attendance clause Mario was said to want if the paying customers at the Civic Arena exceeded 10,000 — a nearly 50 percent increase over 1983-84 — but Perno denies that was a big item on their agenda. "When the money wasn't there the night before the draft we threw in an attendance clause to try to get the dollars up. It wasn't a big deal."

It had been a very tough year, but for Mario — still 112 days shy of his nineteenth birthday, with the summer ahead, a new girlfriend, the lovely Nathalie Asselin, and some real money to spend — life had never looked rosier.

The first item on his agenda was to buy his father, Jean-Guy, a new car. The old family sedan was air-conditioned by a noble collection of rust holes. It was time for a brand-new, bright red Pontiac Parisienne.

As the *Pittsburgh Press* proclaimed on the front page on June 15, 1984, "Glory Days Ahead."

CHAPTER FIVE
Making It in the NHL

*"What he says, he means. Mario is the first guy since
Guy Lafleur who, if he says something, won't change tomorrow.
He's a real man, not afraid to say what he's thinking."*
— Montreal journalist Tom Lapointe

Lapointe is far from the first to draw the comparison between the two greatest Québecois hockey players of this generation. Superficially there are many parallels, despite the fact that Guy's game is blazing speed and Mario's is anticipation and puck control.

Both players were sensational juniors idolized in their home province. But while Guy nearly drowned in adulation — the girls lined up, and the restaurateurs in Quebec City offered free meals for every goal he scored — Mario always had detractors. He could score 11 points in a game and somebody would always remember another game where they claimed he hadn't tried. And when the girls lined up for Mario, though he delighted in the attention as Guy had, he looked uncomfortable and ducked out the side door.

One sure sign of the different way the two players were perceived is the approach of the Canadiens. Years before Guy's 1971 draft year, Sam Pollock, schemed and connived to make sure Montreal had a shot at picking first that year. As the year went on he "gave away" Ralph Backstrom to strengthen LA so that the California Seals would remain in the cellar. Montreal owned the Seals first pick and Pollock would pay whatever price necessary to get the much-coveted Flower.

But when Mario came along with junior stats even better than Guy's, the Canadiens of 13 years later spent more time denigrating than praising the young Quebecois superstar. There was one half-hearted attempt to get an early draft pick in 1984, but the best they could do was Hartford, fifth pick overall — nowhere near high enough to get Mario.

So when the two young men arrived on the doorstep of the NHL, Guy in 1971 and Mario in 1984, they arrived from quite different quarters and with radically disparate mental landscapes.

For one thing, their family lives, beyond the fact that both were born of women named Pierrette, were dramatically different. Lemieux was the cherished centerpiece of his family. Lafleur was set apart from his parents and four sisters

by his great talent. At 14 he was already hundreds of miles from his Thurso, P.Q. (near Ottawa) home playing in Quebec City.

For Guy the commitment and support of the Montreal organization were his foundation. For Mario it was family loyalty he built on. Inevitably Lafleur's reputation was as a team man while Lemieux was considered the individual talent.

And when Mario stepped on the ice for his NHL debut during his very first shift he got a goal. From the beginning he was Le Magnifique. Lafleur struggled, misfired and watched his confidence evaporate through four seasons before he was transformed into Le Demon Blond. (Actually in 1974 he was stung by cries of cowardice, which made him fling off his protective helmet and take charge of himself.)

Mario was always in charge of himself. Too much so, said the critics who pushed the "Coach Killer" line. In his first season the criticism was never his talent but always his character. Behind their hands — or on national television — they'd accuse him of having trouble keeping his head in the game. When he sounded off about coach Bob Berry not taking advantage of line changes, the NHL brain trust looked at each other and nodded knowingly. This kid needed to be taken down a peg or two.

Tough-guy hockey commentator Don Cherry was among the first to take dead aim. On national TV he annointed Mario the "biggest floater in the league."

It was just the kind of spur Mario needed to get hyped for the All-Star Game. He admits he was nervous playing for the first time with champions like Gretzky and Messier. But he also had something to prove. And prove it he did. He scored twice, got one assist and skated away with MVP honors. In the process the Wales Conference trounced Gretzky's Campbell Conference. Afterward a delighted Lemieux went on national television and dedicated the game to Cherry.

Round one to Mr. Lemieux.

The MVP prize of a Chevy Blazer 4x4 went to Mario's brother, Richard, who was then working as a clerk in a grocery store and didn't have much hope of getting a car of his own. Mario and his clan were following in the Gretzky mode.

But the kudos for grace regularly bestowed on The Great One were much more elusive than hockey honors for Mario Lemieux. Both on and off the rink the enigmatic rookie was losing to Lafleur and Gretzky in the public-relations sweepstakes. He was a "brooding presence" and his play "ponderous and slow," closely resembling the "docking of the QE II," one writer pronounced.

When the column appeared in Canada's *Globe and Mail*, with its nation-wide circulation, Mario's rookie season was barely three months old. Still the criticism rolled off his ample shoulders; he was in no danger of losing his faith in himself. Besides, ocean liners and brooding presences don't often wind up, as he did, with the Calder Trophy as the best rookie in the NHL and only the third in history to score 100 points.

There were other histrionics in this memorable season. Mario was the magician who turned veteran also-ran Warren Young into a million-dollar man. Young had been drafted in 1975 by the California Golden Seals but had never been able to make the NHL. Nearly a decade later he was still digging in the corners in the minor leagues.

The Penguins believed Young's dedication and work ethic would be a good influence on Mario, so they brought him up to the majors full-time. Despite a 10-year age difference the two roomed together, played on the same line and became excellent friends. Into the bargain Young scored 40 goals, made 32 assists and the rookie All-Star team. Never mind that his birth certificate said he was 30 years old.

They were a "magic act," said Jim Christie of the *Globe and Mail*, but "Mario was the magician." Young was simply "the poor blighter who got sawed in half."

In the summer of 1985 when the Detroit Red Wings were handing out money trying to buy respectability through free agency, Young was the recipient of their largesse. He signed a long-term million-dollar contract that had him earning twice Mario's 1985 base salary of $125,000.

"I can't blame him for getting what he could," Mario told the press later in the year as Badali sought a new deal with DeBartolo. "I'm happy for him. He got a good contract and some security."

But before his rookie year was well and truly over, before he could bask in the silver glow of the Calder Trophy, Mario had one more hurdle to overcome. Once again international hockey would test his patriotism and dedication to the game. He may have played at a Superman clip all year pulling off his own and Warren Young's magic act, but that would not be enough. Now, because Pittsburgh had not made the playoffs he was expected in Prague to help bolster the Canadian fortunes against the powerful Soviets and Finns.

He didn't want to go.

The list of persuaders is long and impressive. Alan Eagleson, mastermind of the project, EJ, his mentor at Pittsburgh, Gus Badali, his agent, even his hero, Guy Lafleur, talked to him about it. In the end the persuasion and the memory of the controversy over his refusal to go to Sweden at Christmas in 1983 overcame his resistance. Eagleson would later call it one of the two "most successful" negotiations he'd ever done in a career built on that skill.

According to his pal Warren Young, Lemieux resisted because he was tired

and homesick. All he wanted was to get back to Ville Emard. The year had been tumultuous both on and off the ice.

Although his English had improved enormously through a winter spent in careful attention to American soaps, he still found it difficult. He longed to get home to a language and life that would not challenge him.

He'd submitted to more pressure than most rookies could imagine but now, he felt, it should be over. He dreamed of the golf course and Pierrette's home cooking.

But the insatiable hockey baron demanded more. Not surprisingly Mario felt used and frustrated.

In Prague he never warmed up to the project. To make matters worse a nagging groin pull started acting up. Now, not only was he somewhere he didn't want to be, having other people pull the strings, but he couldn't even get the sense of dominance, clarity and control that could usually soothe him out on the ice. Instead there was more frustration as he sat on the bench and watched Team Forgotten struggle.

Pat Riggin, the Washington Capital goalie, had this to say about the team: "We're the lunch-bucket gang — 22 guys who probably have never won anything since peewee hockey, and most of us will never win anything again."

Meanwhile the incomparable Mario was sitting astride the bench on the sidelines drowning in misery. "I've never been hurt very much so it was very difficult to deal with," he told reporters in Prague.

Bob Perno remembers the homesick 19-year-old calling from Prague at three in the morning hoping his agent would be able to pull the strings necessary to bring him home. Perno counseled him to stay and make the best of it.

After three days in Europe he announced publicly he wanted to go home. It was time for Eagleson's second-most successful feat of negotiation. Into the mix he threw his highly developed sense of gamesmanship. With coach Doug Carpenter and team captain Rick Vaive's help, Eagleson bamboozled the street-smart Mario. First they told him he should indeed go home because he was a "poison" on the team. Next they told him they couldn't get him a flight out for several more days.

Mario's misery was now shot through with anger. He boiled as he watched another first round 4-2 loss to the United States. Between periods he grabbed the Eagle's elbow and announced he would stay. The Canadians were immediately contenders.

"I was really down," he explained later. "But the bad feelings went away when I got back in the lineup against Finland and was able to contribute by scoring an important goal."

His talent was almost enough to net the Canadians a gold medal. They narrowly lost to Finland in the gold-medal round and came home with silver, the best world championship showing since 1962 and the silver-medal performance of the Galt Terriers.

Team Forgotten's medal was described as a "stunning upset," properly laid at the feet of Mario, le Magnifique. He warmed to the praise. "Doing this is a greater thrill than I ever dreamed of," he told one reporter. "Of course I would come here again," he told another.

And after it was all toted up the pundits pronounced Mario's first NHL year "sensational."

The same adjective could be applied to the Penguins' business triumph. When owner Edward J. DeBartolo signed Mario he told the media, "This is the greatest thing to happen to this franchise since its inception."

He went on to predict the team would be competitive within two years. He was dead on. Two years later the team had doubled its point production. And more importantly to the money men, attendance immediately jumped an astounding 46 percent to more than 10,000 Steel City souls.

As Eddie Johnston had told the naysayers at the Memorial Cup the year before, Mario Lemieux was indeed a player "to hang your hat on."

CHAPTER SIX
Second Best?

"No player — not Wayne Gretzky, not Bobby Orr — has ever
been asked to do so much both on the ice and off. No player
has ever responded more brilliantly and gracefully."
— *Sports Illustrated* on Lemieux in his second season

In the early 80s, if there was one incontrovertible tenet of hockey wisdom it was this: Gretzky was the nonpareil; the sport would never see his like again.

And then, when the Great One was only 25 years old, the contender strolled in.

Throughout his second year, reporters constantly quizzed Lemieux on his chances of passing his hero. The question came up more often than anyone intended because Lemieux was so laconic. They'd pepper him on the fine points of the game or about his attitude to this or that, but eventually they'd run out of steam, defeated by his resolutely monosyllabic answers. They'd fall back on the question of Gretzky. The subject, they knew, was usually good for a sentence or two. This was something the big man felt deeply about.

"I think I can pass him," was Mario's standard reply. "Not this year or next, but it will happen." Oddly nobody took this extraordinary claim as a boast. It was simply Mario's supreme self-confidence asserting itself. Whether he could actually deliver on the claim was something else again.

As Mario established himself in the NHL his awe of Gretzky diminished as his admiration for him grew. Nobody but these two knows better the demands superstardom places on a young man's character.

Mario, shy and reticent on most topics, would launch into 30-word sentences when the opportunity to pay tribute to Gretzky arose. In December of his third season in the NHL he told Bill Houston of the *Globe and Mail* about the first time they played golf together in a celebrity tournament. (Mario won the tournament. Gretzky's game was passable.)

At the time Mario was a lanky unproven 16-year-old. Gretzky, at 21, was already a bona fide hero. "He had all kinds of money, all kinds of success but he was staying on the ground," Mario remembered. "I thought to myself that's the way a hockey player should be."

But by his second and third years in the NHL Mario was rapidly gaining assurance while Gretzky was enduring a bit of a rough patch in what had been an ice-smooth career. In 1985-86 The Great One scored 215 points in a tour-de-force year that made history. But although the Oilers finished first overall by a wide margin, they were knocked out in the division finals by Calgary and were on the golf links by April 30, 24 days before the Canadiens carried home the Stanley Cup.

The next year Mario steadily improved, challenging his hero for the first time in both production and popularity. In their most publicized matchup of the season on January 22, 1987, Lemieux outdazzled Gretzky and led his team to a 7-4 victory over the Oilers. With one goal and four assists he was first star of the game. Gretzky with two assists was third star, and when he skated out to take a bow a few hundred of the fickle Edmonton crowd booed him.

At the same time balloting was fast and furious over who should play at Rendez-Vous '87, Marcel Aubut's flashy tribute to international hockey. In the end Gretzky was the second center losing to Mario in the fans' popularity vote by 35,000 votes. "Maybe they're tired of Wayne Gretzky winning things," Mario told reporters.

And at the end of the year the players' vote for the Lester B. Pearson Award to the league's "most outstanding player" went to Mario, too. He had scored 74 fewer points and had failed in his desperate bid to yank the Penguins into the playoffs, but still the players recognized his quality.

Gretzky, always resolutely gracious, was hurt, insiders said. "The *media* have always been fair to me," he said as he collected the Hart Trophy for an unprecedented eighth year in a row. The league's MVP is decided on a vote by the Professional Hockey Writers Association.

But the message was clear: the contender had flexed his considerable muscle and the competition was on in earnest.

During those first two years of establishing himself in the league, Mario never ducked comparisons with Gretzky or questions about his own intensity. His line was modest but straightforward. Gretzky is "unbelievable in intensity," he'd say and then add,"I know I have the potential and talent. It's just a matter of working hard every night, as Gretzky does. He works hard every shift, giving all he's got. I know that's what I've got to do."

Mario also conceded dominance to Gretzky in two other areas — passing and skating. But not all pundits — or players — even then agreed about the skating. Mario's long strides don't look as quick. But they take him farther and faster than Gretzky's elbow-flapping rushes, players who've shared the same ice surface say.

But in the most important quality of their greatness both Gretzky and Lemieux seem evenly matched. They have "eyes on their sticks," as the Oiler GM Glen Sather puts it.

In this Mario concedes nothing. "I think I can read the play as well as him. I think my anticipation is as good."

Students of the game say the two have an unprecedented peripheral vision that allows them to see the whole ice surface as if they were sitting up in the broadcast booth.

Others talk about the speed with which the messages are translated from brains to hands while lesser players are still registering the position of the puck. "It's a gift of God," says former Pittsburgh scout Albert Mandanici. "Where else could it come from?"

But Mario, despite the occasional handicap of a phlegmatic temperament, has one extra great gift Gretzky can never acquire. Size. For all his magic, Wayne doesn't quite reach the six-foot mark the handbooks peg him at. Mario at six-foot four and one-half inches and 212 pounds is half a foot taller and 42 pounds heavier. He can, when the magical connections are made, charge through the opposition and leave bodies flying in his wake. Gretzky is defter, more circuitous and less dangerous.

Yet as the two superheroes finished the 1987 season and headed into the Canada Cup, it was still very much Gretzky's decade. All Mario's promise could do was raise the specter of the passing of the guard.

"Everybody knows that Gretzky is the best player in the world," said Mario's boss, Penguin GM Eddie Johnston in 1987, shrugging off the interminable comparisons. "But there is nothing wrong with our club having the second best."

He may have been the contender in league terms but in Pittsburgh Mario Lemieux was king. "Le Roi de Pittsburgh," the Montreal dailies proclaimed. At first he'd perched at the edge of Pittsburgh life, homesick and embarrassed by his English. But living with Tom and Nancy Mathews and their three grown sons, he'd gradually acquired a taste for the city said to be one of the most livable in America.

Pittsburgh was enjoying a renaissance of civic pride, and Mario was ideally situated to ride the crest of its new spirit. After the first summer he didn't go back to Montreal, where he was more likely to be recognized and hounded.

He was now much more comfortable in English, having taken a crash course by living in an English-speaking home and watching the afternoon soaps religiously. *One Life to Live* was one of the best he remembers. "On a soap opera they talk real clear," he told *Playboy* magazine in an unlikely interview in 1989. His favorite television pastime was watching reruns of *Three's Company*. "I don't like to watch hockey on television," he tells interviewers. "I've seen enough games."

In his second year he moved into a bachelor apartment, but stayed close to the Mathews because Nancy was "like having another mother. She still comes over all the time, cleans and brings over food. And she does my mail." Pittsburgh was becoming home, right down to the coddling family environment.

By his third year he'd really settled in. His Montreal girlfriend, Nathalie Asselin, had finished college and joined him. They moved into a house and started planning the 16- or 18-room mansion in the suburban hills of Mount Lebanon where they would finally move in the spring of 1989.

Even with the vivacious Nathalie by his side Mario still led an exceedingly quiet life. "She takes nothing like the role Vikki Moss (Gretzky's previous girl-friend) took in Edmonton," say Mario's friends. "He prefers her not to work." So she plays tennis with the players' wives and looks after the house and Mario's morale."

She, too, protects and coddles, screening his calls and taking care of him however she can.

"She's great," says Bob Perno. "She's bubbly and fun, definitely part of the reason Mario has done so well."

The pair were introduced when they were 17 by a mutual cousin, Stephane Lemieux. Nathalie claims she was immediately smitten. Mario isn't saying. But the fact is, although there may have been flings, she is his first and only girl-friend.

Out in company Mario and Nathalie cut a striking figure. With heels Asselin is six feet tall and gives away nothing to Janet Jones in the beauty department. But with Mario, she shares an interest in a quiet life away from the limelight. "If you see Mario in a nightclub, you can bet he's there to make a phone call," says an amused Dave Molinari of the *Pittsburgh Press*.

Molinari uses Gustave Flaubert's injunction to be "orderly and regular in your daily life so you can be violent and original in your work" to describe Mario's life-style. The Pittsburgh columnist longs for a little flamboyance in the city's hero, but he does not buy the "Big Goof" label with which some of the writers tagged Mario in his first two years, as he struggled with the language.

Molinari accepts Mario's belief that he must husband his immense talent to perform at the level he's expected. He's watched Mario avoid the party scene that so adversely affected Pierre Larouche, another Quebec phenom slated to save the franchise. In Pittsburgh it's well known Mario avoids the bar scene and speaks out against drugs and alcohol.

"We couldn't play hockey if we took drugs," Mario explained in his *Playboy* interview. "The game's too fast — we couldn't survive. Alcohol is a little bit different. There are guys in the NHL who like to go out after a game and drink five, six, seven, eight beers. It's a way to unwind, and it makes you go to bed a little earlier. That's the main reason."

But while Mario continued to espouse the simple life there were small signs he had begun to acquire a taste for at least the Pittsburgh version of the good life. The Mathews, a wealthy family, set the tone. First his American cars gave

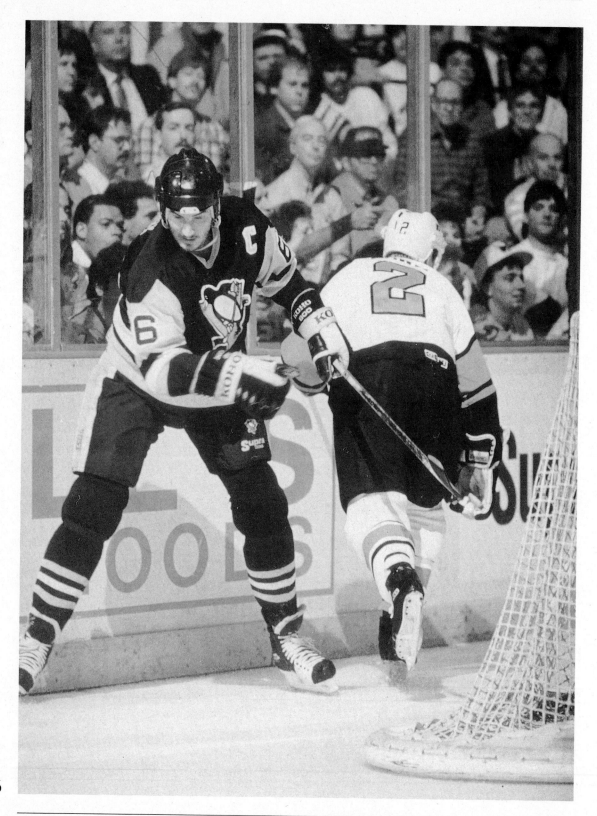

way to luxury European models. During the end of his third year in Pittsburgh, he was debating whether he should trade in his Mercedes for a BMW.

He started to talk about collecting wine, even bought books on the subject and planned an extensive wine cellar for his new home. Now when he came home to Ville Emard, Pierrette was suddenly nervous about which wine to serve with dinner.

Among the friends he'd left behind in Montreal there was talk — slightly incredulous talk — of his flashy diamond ring emblazoned with his number, 66. The neigborhood buzzed with talk of the "palace" he was building in Pittsburgh.

Nobody missed the pride and concern he was lavishing on the construction of the new house. The project ended up taking two years, with several detours into the courts — one because the roughed-in doorways were only six feet high. The master of the house had to duck to get through them.

Mario, says Bob Perno, is a product of his family — easygoing, laid-back, with very little interest in pushing himself to the limit. When the bonanza of a giant NHL contract befell their son he was more than willing to share his wealth with the family. But they didn't want a new home, they said. His parents and brother saw no reason to move from their comfortable six-room Ville Emard flat. (Money seduces gradually, though, for by 1989 Pierrette would at least be mulling over the idea of moving.)

But Pierrette watched her boy living thousands of miles away, in a different culture, and by a different value system and forging a new American life. There, a grand home was one of the most significant symbols of success. Mario had to have one.

In the summer of 1987, Mario's main off-ice preoccupation continued to be golf. There were charity tournaments, celebrity pro-ams and a daily round to keep his edge. His friends marveled at how good he was, at how quickly he was improving. By 1988 his handicap was down to three or four. Those who saw him play were saying he might indeed, if he is still interested, be able to make the PGA tour when he finishes hockey.

Pittsburgh continues its love affair with the talented center. When Mayor Sophie Masloff appeared on Pat Sajak's CBS talk show in 1989 she received a gift — a replica of Mario's hockey sweater. It was a fitting symbol. Mario is a nationally recognized Pittsburgh icon and one of their most bankable commodities.

Poll after poll in Pittsburgh votes him the most popular figure in the city, the most eligible bachelor, the best-loved sports figure, even the Dapper Dan Man of the Year. No matter that the Penguins have only made it to the playoffs once since he arrived. There has been no cooling of their ardor.

In 1985-86 for example, when Mario was languishing a distant second behind Gretzky in the scoring race, the Sold Out sign was going up with some regularity in the Civic Arena for the first time in years.

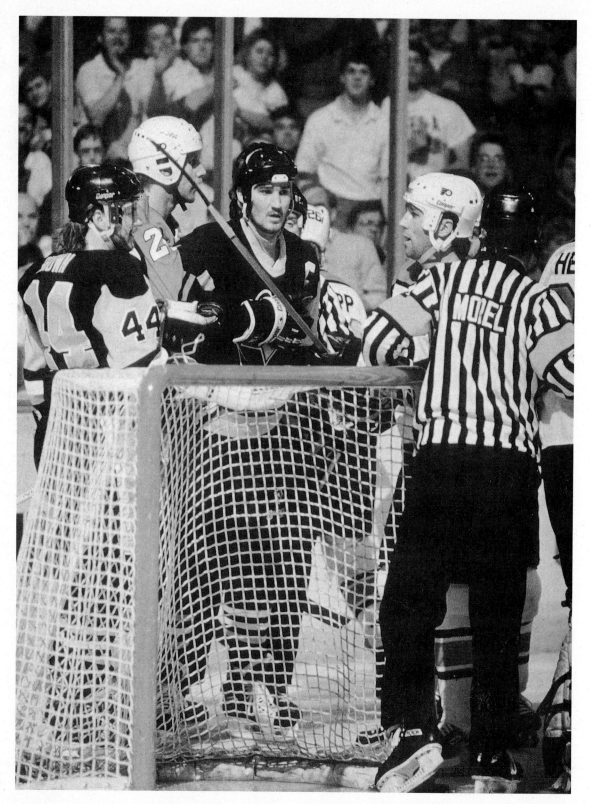

Mario, then in his second year, claimed he was playing 20 to 30 percent better than the year before. The whole team was suddenly a contender — at least for a playoff spot. The talk of moving the franchise to Hamilton, Ontario, had abruptly died. "The Franchise," everybody knew, was building a big house in the hills and fixing to stay.

By April, 1987, Pittsburgh was in a dogfight with the Rangers for the final playoff spot. Mario, who had carried the team, was rundown and suffering from bronchitis. He spent the last weekend before the final game in the hospital. Once again because of the vagaries of the playoff system, Pittsburgh, fourteenth overall, did not make the playoffs, while teams with much-worse records survived for another round or two.

Mario took it hard. His bronchitis and his disappointment combined to keep him away from the World Championship once again. Again the collective fury of the international hockey cadre rained down on him. Again he stood his ground.

He had plenty to be satisfied with. Over the past three years his accomplishments were outstanding. He'd turned on a whole city to hockey. (Average attendance in Pittsburgh had more than doubled, from under 7000 to over 15,000.) Personally he'd grown beyond his "point-scoring machine" reputation into a fine two-way player. And into the bargain he'd become a pretender to the throne of the greatest player in the history of the game.

Not bad for a 21-year-old.

And the best was yet to come.

CHAPTER SEVEN
Canada Cup: the Measuring Rod

"This is a personal challenge for me. It's another step in my career, a great chance to show what I can do."
— Mario Lemieux, before the Canada Cup, September 1987

Nobody could have predicted that Lemieux, whose ledger was filled with black marks for turning down invitations to play for Team Canada, would emerge as the leader in the 1987 Canada Cup.

Nobody, that is, except the wizards of the game like Canadian and Soviet team captains, respectively Wayne Gretzky and Viatcheslav Fetisov. Both saw the future of the sport in the young French Canadian. They glimpsed the fire in his eye and knew that something had awakened the sleeping giant.

Gretzky's tribute was the more surprising. "With Team Canada Mario picked everybody up, including me," said Gretzky. "He'll do the same in the NHL."

Fetisov remembered the youngster, from the 1985 World Championship, who had skated through his team and powered the Canadians to an upset silver medal. "Someday, it (the best player) will be Mario Lemieux," he said a fortnight before the first puck was dropped.

He couldn't have predicted how soon the someday would arrive.

During that nine-game tournament the magic that ignited Lemieux fired up his teammates. Suddenly everybody was outreaching themselves. Lemieux led the way, scoring 11 goals including four game-winners. Gretzky, the playmaker, had assists on nine of Lemieux's goals. And in the Dream Final against the Soviets, with Mario scoring three goals in game 2 and the winning goal in game 3, the pair looked as if they had been created to play together, so great was their synergism — coach Mike Keenan's word for the magic of their combination. Center Doug Gilmour was more earthy. "Those two together are scary," he said with awe in his voice.

But Gretzky said it best and most completely: "Mario and I were playing out of instinct. We think the same things, go to the same holes, see everything the same way."

In the end Mario would collect 18 points, Gretzky 21. After it was over, The

Great One quietly admitted he had never played better. The joy that gripped the dressing room after the final defeat of the Soviets was streaked with sorrow: the best series in which they'd ever played was over; there was little chance of seeing its like again.

As Mario had been acutely aware, this was his opportunity to shine. Playing in relative obscurity in Pittsburgh had been the perfect incubation for his skills. The Canada Cup came at a time when, as he said, "I was ready for a challenge."

In the second game of the final with the Soviets, the Game of the Century, as some had called it, there was time somewhere between the first and second overtime periods for Lemieux to slip into his Superman cape. When the puck dropped he was ready. Ready to score the winning goal in the best game anyone can ever remember.

And for all the doubters who had insisted Mario could never dig deep enough to put two extraordinary games together back to back, Mario returned a couple of nights later to again score the game-winner. The faithful hanging from the rafters in the temple that had once been Copps Coliseum pounded out an ovation that rocked the southern Ontario city of Hamilton.

The two teams were evenly matched, but in the end the series belonged to Canada — just as the upcoming year would soon belong to Mario.

CHAPTER EIGHT
The Arrival

*"I got a lot of confidence from this (Canada Cup). You learn a
lot about what to say in the dressing room between periods if
you're down two or three goals. We had a lot of guys there
who won Stanley Cups there. I just listened to them."*
— Mario Lemieux

The year of 1987-88 was a significant watershed for Mario. Dressed in the luster of the Canada Cup, he had definitely arrived. The fans had finally understood his value and he had finally grasped his responsibilities.

Gordie Howe, usually the soul of generosity, had remarked once that he'd seen Mario play a "lot of five-minute games. And win them in those five minutes." After the Canada Cup Howe added, "He doesn't take nights off anymore."

Rocket Richard had praised his talent but questioned the "fire in his belly."

Now Mario, about to turn 22, had breathed deeply the air of intensity in the Team Canada dressing room. He'd glimpsed the depths to which champions like Messier and Gretzky would dig for greatness. When he skated out for the first face-off of the regular season, he knew what was required of a hockey great.

"Every shift Wayne tried to do the impossible," Mario later marveled to *Sports Illustrated*.

It had always been difficult to get Mario to work out during the off-season, but this year because of the six weeks of Canada Cup his conditioning was excellent. He'd been a half-a-pack-a-day smoker; now he gave it up. He'd been content to roll along as the cream of the Pittsburgh crop with occasional one-on-one matchups with Gretzky. Now he lusted for overall dominance.

"I am not admitting I ever doubted myself," he said as the season got under way and his magnificent skill became more and more apparent, "but there was a time when I wasn't sure I could be a great hockey player. I thought I was a good hockey player, but a good player is not a great one.

"Just being with all those terrific players was an inspiration. I'm sure that was when I really reached the peak of my game."

Now having understood his own potential, he went about making sure everyone else did, too.

Two circumstances conspired to help him. On November 24, Paul Coffey, the best offensive defenceman in the league was traded to the Penguins after an acrimonious contract dispute. Nobody knew it yet, but the dismantling of the Oiler dynasty was beginning. In Coffey, Gretzky's loss was Mario's most decided gain.

"There's a big difference when Paul is playing," he explained after a month with his new teammate. "It gives me a lot more open ice because guys can't key in on one player anymore. It really helps on the power play because now I don't have to come all the way back. Paul just feeds it up to me."

As the old year wore out, there was a second circumstance that would ultimately push Lemieux into the winner's circle. Gretzky sprained his right knee. He would be out for 16 games, the longest interruption ever in a Gretzky season.

In eight previous years Wayne had missed a total of eight games. Now his enforced rest would have everybody speculating that Mario would beat him to the Art Ross Trophy for most points in the season. Papers like the *Toronto Sun* started keeping charts on "the Champion" and "the Challenger," projecting their April totals from their January pace.

On February 9 the All-Star game convened in St. Louis without Gretzky.

Mario sizzled with three assists and three goals, including the game-winner in overtime. Mario's clear dominance startled the hockey world. Would the race turn into an unbecoming rout?

Not a rout. The demigod would not be humiliated. Gretzky came back after the All-Star break, but the scoring title was beyond reach. On the final night of the regular season Mario had 168 points to Gretzky's 149. The pundits pronounced it Gretzky's "worst" season.

Future historians of the game will pick through the detritus of March and April, 1988, and see the subtle signs of the passing of an era. Some of that was clear in the way endorsements started to flow Mario's way as the season wore on. His total income from endorsements hovered around $200,000, scarcely a tenth of Gretzky's estimated $2-million. But for a player who had been denigrated as lazy and unpatriotic the new interest showed a remarkably renovated image. Mario, for all his reticence, for all his shunning the limelight, was becoming the second-most-sought-after player in the NHL, slightly ahead of the loquacious Lanny McDonald.

The Penguins finished twelfth overall with 81 points, their best season of the decade. But once again the strength of their Patrick Division shut them out of post-season competition. Mario was pensioned off to the golf links while Gretzky,

now rested from his enforced layoff, was magnificent, leading his team to yet another Stanley Cup.

But when Awards night rolled around the fabulous Gretzky was shut out. He didn't even show up at a ceremony he had dominated for the eight previous years. "There was no reason to be there," Gretzky explained. "People will always say things and have their opinions, but the bottom line is there was no need to be there, so I didn't go."

"It was definitely his (Lemieux's) day. He had a tremendous season. There was no need to take anything away from Mario. He was a very deserving winner."

Mario glistened, paying gracious tribute to Gretzky and demonstrating in the process the kind of modesty one expects from a world-class 22-year-old.

"I thought it was about time this year that I started to show my stuff," he told the world. "It started at the Canada Cup, playing with Wayne. I learned a lot from him. In my opinion he's still the best in the world. It's just too bad he had the injury. But I was lucky enough to take advantage of it."

He won every award he was eligible for by whopping margins and into the bargain collected a clutch of trucks that he would distribute among his family. Unquestionably, of all the honors in this most decorated year, the prize that meant the most was the Hart Trophy, for the most valuable player. Gretzky's name was engraved on that very special piece of silverware eight times, once for every year he had been in the league.

Now, Mario must have assumed, the Lemieux years had begun.

It was not to be.

First there was the Wedding of the Century. Gretzky and his bride, Hollywood starlet Janet Jones, added considerable luster to the NHL by staging a 700-guest extravaganza in Edmonton. There were breathless daily reports on everything from the price of the champagne to Janet's $40,000 gown. As the media hysteria mounted the Wedding began to rival the lavish nuptial productions of English royalty.

Mario and Nathalie were not among the select 700.

Scarcely had the wedding hype cleared the news pages when a much more dramatic story broke. Oiler owner, Peter Pocklington, had traded Gretzky to the L.A. Kings for a few players and a wad of cash fat enough to choke a horse. Gretzky signed an eight-year $20-million deal with Bruce McNall.

Sitting at home in Pittsburgh, Lemieux must have smiled broadly. The Trade of the Century would have significant impact on his own contract negotiations, which were, at the moment, rudderless. But even more than the dollars and cents it would mean in his pocket, Gretzky's move to the Kings was important because it would level the playing field between the two supernovas of the league. How good would Gretzky be without the Oilers? Everybody wondered. But Mario, especially, ached to find out.

He exploded into the 1988-89 season with the same zest he'd shown in the 1988 All-Star game. In the first dozen games of the season he collected 41 points. It was the best start in the history of the game. Pundits talked of the possibility of a 300-point season.

It was a perfect milieu for Tom Reich, Mario's new hotshot agent, to get down to negotiating the new contract. Obviously when Wayne's new numbers were announced, the jolt was felt through the whole league. Mario's demands shot up. He wanted to be in the same tax bracket as Gretzky. Maybe not quite $2-million a year, but close.

Despite protracted talks and Mario's obvious value to the team no agreement was reached. There was a new figure in the piece. Eddie Johnston was being eased out by the DeBartolos in favor of family friend Tony Esposito. Espo had taken over effective control of the club after he was named VP and GM over Johnston's head on April 14, 1988.

The move was a blow to Mario, who had been close to Johnston ever since the days of his disappointing Memorial Cup four years — and half a lifetime — ago.

"I knew the handwriting was on the wall for Johnston when they (the DeBartolos) stepped in and blocked the trade for Andy Moog," said one long-time insider. Although Johnston would hang around for another year before

moving on to Hartford, he was essentially powerless. Mario felt the chill winds of change, especially when another of his close friends, scout Albert Mandanici, was abruptly fired before June was out.

Was Mario, despite the hockey accolades, the fabulous attendance records and his obvious appeal in Pittsburgh, being isolated? Was his fierce independence and sense of his own worth causing consternation in the owner's suite? It was too soon to say, except that the horizon looked a little more clouded than it had in the past.

The issue of Guy Lafleur was one more warning sign of trouble. When Guy decided in the summer of 1988 to make a comeback, Pittsburgh was one of the first teams he called. Lafleur did not underestimate the value in point-totals and pleasure of playing with a talent like Lemieux. Mario was thrilled at the prospect of playing with his former idol.

In the end, although Tony Esposito professed interest, "he didn't phone back," says Lafleur. "He didn't really pursue it."

Esposito's brother Phil, GM of the Rangers, on the other hand, wanted to talk dollars and cents immediately.

"In two hours of talking we had worked out the contract we would sign if I made it the team," Lafleur explains.

"Well yes, I would have liked to play with Mario," Lafleur concedes now. "I would have got more points. But I was happy to play for the Rangers and I wanted to sign the first acceptable contract."

Mario, friends say, was unhappy about the way the Lafleur approach had been treated. He sensed a failure of respect. His own contract talks were in shambles, having now dragged on for months. Both sides agreed they should have a long-term deal à la Gretzky. The only trouble was they were millions of dollars apart in what they thought the contract should be worth.

Finally Mario lost patience. They set a November deadline, which came and went with no resolution. Finally on November 30, 1988, after a five-hour session with DeBartolo they settled on a one-year deal for $1.9-million (Cdn). The talks on the long-term contract would be deferred until the summer so that Mario could be free to concentrate on hockey.

Speculation was rife that Mario and Tony were at loggerheads. The much-heralded former goalie was now handling the team's finances "as if each Penguin dollar were the last in his personal bank account," claimed the *Toronto Sun*'s Jim O'Leary. Certainly it was true that parsimony is not a quality becoming a billionaire listed twenty-fourth on *Forbes* list of the world's wealthiest men.

Meanwhile Mario continued his relentless attack on the scoring records. Bob Perno remembers meeting Gretzky in Quebec early in the season. "He was already saying that Mario would be tough to catch because he had opened up such a big lead."

As the season wore on the tributes poured in. Canadian Press named him male athlete of the year. But even more of an honor was this assessment from Gordie Howe: "He's unbelievably good now, and we don't know how good he will be."

While the speculation raged that this year "le mieux" (the best) might indeed live up to his name, Mario outmaneuvered, outdeked and outwitted everyone who tried to take the puck from him. There were games that dazzled in their purity, such as the 8-6 defeat of the New Jersey Devils where Mario scored five goals — each one in a different situation — one a power-play goal, one a shorthanded goal, one a penalty shot, one in regulation play and the final one into the open net.

But the streak cooled as the new year wore on. In the All-Star game, where he'd shone the year before, he was curiously lackluster, netting only one assist, while Gretzky led the Campbell conference to a 9-5 win with one goal and two assists.

He seemed even more remote. There were fewer and fewer public appearances. It was harder to get an interview with Mario Lemieux than with any other player in the league.

In March the simmering dispute with the media finally erupted. Gary Green, TSN commentator, lashed out at the press insisting Mario was unworthy of MVP honors because he wouldn't promote the game. Green was furious because Mario had stood up The Sports Network twice for scheduled interviews. Penguins' Public Relations Director Cindy Himes insists it was all a misunderstanding. Still the impression of petulance persisted.

Green claimed Lemieux's only public appearance for months was for a potato-chip company. "And he got 10 grand for that!" Green snapped.

With the Canada Cup Mario appeared to have redeemed himself in international hockey; now there was a new rap on him. Green and others dismiss Mario's contention that he needs his privacy. "I figure he makes $2-million a year for more than just playing hockey," Green says.

But for Mario the irritated reporters were no more than gnats buzzing around his head. The team had slowed to a walk once March rolled around bringing with it tightened defensive play throughout the league. The Penguins were assured of a playoff spot — more than could be said of the past seven seasons — but still the prognosis did not look good.

They were slumping and acutely feeling their lack of experience. Last year's league MVP had never played in an NHL playoff game.

Unfortunately it showed. Memories of the miserable 1984 Memorial Cup were soon to flood in.

The first disappointment came with Lemieux's 199-point total in the scoring race. Where once a few months ago they had been talking 300, now he was gunning for 200. And although he would be only the second player in history to go so far, the edge was off the accomplishment. He strafed the net in the final six games and came up with a 13-goal total. Still one point shy of his goal.

With that sticking in his craw he headed into the playoffs, for him the real point of the exercise. Beside the holy grail of the Stanley Cup all else paled.

In the first round they faced the New York Rangers, a team that had lost its blustery competitive edge, a team that had managed to lose 12 of its last 15 games. Three games before the end of the season, their coach was another casualty — GM Phil Esposito fired Michel Bergeron and put himself behind the bench. The Rangers lost every game Phil coached — the last three and then four straight to the Penguins.

Mario hadn't distinguished himself in the series. In triumphing over such demoralized opposition the team had hardly covered themselves in glory. Quibbles, my dear. Pittsburgh had won!

It was only the third time in franchise history the team had won a round of the playoffs. Steel City fans went mad with delight. They made signs proclaiming Mario for Mayor and readied themselves for the Philadelphia Flyers.

As was his custom Mario was trying to clear his mind for the next level of challenge. He wasn't having much luck; his sandpapery relationship with GM Tony Esposito seemed to be coming to a head.

He didn't understand the way Tony was behaving, and was definitely losing patience. And then there was the matter of security. One night he'd run into a problem with irate Ranger fans as he was leaving Madison Square Gardens. The toughs rocked, kicked and pounded on the taxi, frightening the cabbie and his three celeb fares — Paul Coffey, Mario Lemieux and Jim Johnson. Mario felt the time had come for him to have security for those times that interviews forced him to leave the rink later than his teammates.

According to his friend Tom Lapointe of the *Journal de Montréal*, Mario was disappointed in the way Esposito treated his request. This was one more thing to get straightened out in the summer, he told his friend. Mario was irked that he was being dismissed as a prima donna. "I'd like to be recognized as the hockey player I am," he told Lapointe.

Word around Pittsburgh was that Reich would be negotiating Mario's new contract directly with the team owners, bypassing Espo. As usual the awkward fit of a GM and a superstar with 10 times the salary and influence was raising hackles.

Through this mini-crisis Mario struggled to keep his mind free to engage the Broad Street Bullies of Philadelphia. For a player such as Mario who likes space to play his game, this was to be a particularly trying assignment.

Two games into the series they were tied 1-1. "Lemieux has yet to really get untracked in these playoffs," the critics complained. The problem was the Flyers' huge Swedish defenceman Kjell Samuelsson. At six-foot six and 225 pounds, he's the biggest player in the league, besting Mario by almost two inches and 20 pounds. "He's practically impossible to beat one on one," Mario admitted after the second game, a 4-2 loss.

But it was the fourth game, a humiliating 4-1 loss, where Lemieux's pride took a serious pounding. First he misfired on a superb breakaway opportunity, then he was hurt when Samuelsson cut him down in front of the Philadelphia goal. Finally he had to leave the game with whiplash after a harrowing accidental check by his own teammate Randy Cunneyworth.

"Philly is taking no prisoners out there," quipped an obviously delighted Don Cherry between periods. "Every time he (Mario) touches the puck they're all over him."

By the fifth game, with the series tied 2-2, Mario had been no more than a vague presence. Now with a twisted back and neck from the Cunneyworth check, he was listed as a doubtful starter. For an 85-goal scorer who had publicly proclaimed his hunger for a good playoff Lemieux continued to be a disturbingly pale imitation of his regular-season self. Rumors circulated that his back — a problem that comes and goes with all of the tall rangy Lemieux men — was bothering him. There must be something wrong, the smart money reasoned. And then, abruptly shaking off the back and neck pain, overcoming the problems with turning his head, Mario Lemieux, the doubtful starter, made it clear in the opening seconds of the fifth game that he had come to play.

Associated Press described it as a "Game for the Ages." For the angry, humiliated Lemieux it was a miracle. In the first period he erupted for four goals, an NHL record for speed out of the gate. He finished off the night with a fifth goal and three assists, and the Penguins downed the Flyers 10-7. "It's the best I've ever seen him play," said coach Gene Ubriaco, rubbing his hands.

Everybody expected Mario's switch was now stuck on *go* and the Pens would make short work of the Flyers. But that was without figuring on the Flyers' tenacity and the Lemieux inertia if he has no room to move.

After the sixth game, a 6-2 loss where Mario was held pointless, it did indeed seem that his switch was stuck — but not on *go*. Only nine times throughout the season had he been held pointless. Now it had happened in two out of three games.

The series was a collision of styles — "run and gun" versus "clutch and grab." Everyone knew the seventh game would be decided on which team could force their style on the opponent and make it stick through sixty minutes of hockey.

After the sixth game the Penguins were battered and bloodied. Coffey was the only regular player who showed up for the optional skate the day before the seventh game. Rob Brown spent the day in physio trying to get his damaged leg back in working order.

Mario went underground, giving his pal Lapointe a few quotes for the media and telling everyone he preferred to keep his "head in the game."

The Pittsburgh press billed the game the "most important in the franchise's 21-year-history.

"A win . . . would put the team in the first rank of the National Hockey League teams. A loss and they're just another also-ran and Lemieux is still in Gretzky's shadow."

Superstars aside, the key players in this encounter would be the goalkeepers. (Ron) Hextall the Dangerous was the perfect symbol for the Flyer style. So far he had outshone Tom Barrasso in the nets and used his fabled ferocity to great advantage.

Then just 30 minutes before game seven, Philadelphia announced Ken Wregget, not Hextall, would stand up to the Penguin attack. The Pittsburgh fans hooted with delight as rumor spread like a summer grassfire through the Civic Auditorium. In the press box the hockey writers composed their opening paragraphs for the next day's papers.

The story was simple. Wregget had only played two and a half games in the past two months; he would be blown out by a hyped-up Pittsburgh offence.

But it didn't happen that way. Without their leader in intensity, it was the Philadelphia defence rather than the Pittsburgh offence that was hyped up. Wregget, solid rather than spectacular, withstood the test, blocking 39 Penguin shots. After the first period the Penguins were down 1-0. Don Cherry once again started riding his favorite target. "He's floatin' out there," he shouted at the cameras. "If he doesn't wake up soon, they're gonzo."

"Gonzo" described it exactly. There was a fluttering pulse as Mario came out at the beginning of the second and let one fly past Wregget, but that was the only sign of life. The game ended in a convincing 4-1 win for the Flyers. Mario and his team of "also-rans" headed to the showers for the last time.

Even adding in the "Game for the Ages," it was a disappointing showing for both Lemieux and Coffey. They reacted very differently. For Mario, getting to the seventh game of the second round was an accomplishment to be savored. He wasn't content with the loss, but he said he'd learned the importance of experience. His vast confidence makes him believe they'll be back next year.

"The Flyers showed experience helps," he said after it was over. "We have to maintain a positive outlook. "This is the first time we've been in the playoffs in six (actually seven) years. We have to remember that."

Coffey, who has played on a clutch of Stanley Cup teams in Edmonton, knows just how difficult repeating is. He understands the psychology of winning. You should never say "Next time," he counselled after the loss. Instead a winner thinks, "The time is now."

Mario has a sense of inevitability about the Stanley Cup. "I know I'll drink from that cup one day," he says. "I just know it."

They call him an "individual talent" but not in this. The Stanley Cup is the real test, he knows. Ask Lanny McDonald. Ask any hockey lifer.

Yes, the duel with Gretzky is compelling, but a sterile collection of statistics or even trophies has no magic to compare with a Stanley Cup ring. And there, he still has, he knows, a long way to go.

In 1988-89 he and Gretzky played on teams of similar caliber. But the Gretzky Kings improved from eighteenth to fourth overall. The Penguins finished sixth. Both teams were knocked out in the second round of the playoffs, but the Kings lost to the eventual Stanley Cup champions.

There are still several mountains to climb, a fact that was painfully obvious as the NHL silverware was handed out for 1989. Except for the Art Ross Trophy for leading scorer, Mario was ignored. For all his points, for all his team's dramatically improved record, all he got was a spot on the first All-Star team. The key Hart Trophy went to Wayne. In the balloting Mario was a distant second.

"Nothing in this league makes sense," he said afterward, refusing further comment. When pressed he simply shrugged and added, "The facts are there," in what was described as a mood of petulance.

The problem of the contract and the Espo relationship still hung over him as the season wore itself out. Yes, there would be other years, but even at the tender age of 23, he was beginning to realize that other years would mean other problems. He had tried to bear down and focus only on hockey, but the formula for controlling his destiny had eluded him.

As he headed into the summer of 1989 the fingerprint of his impact on hockey was still very indistinct. But with the pressure finally off he turned to golf.

"I would like to play professionally when this is over," he said. "That is my dream, anyway. There is something clean and bright about golf. It is a game where you are alone and within yourself. That's something I like sometimes, to be alone and to see what is inside myself.

"Sometimes with hockey — although I try not to let it be so — there is not time for reflection. Thinking is important. Thinking what you are."

KAMIN & HOWELL INC.
is one of the world's leading packagers
and publishers of books.
They have produced more than 70 titles.